The
59-Second
Employee

The
59-Second
Employee

*How to Stay One Second Ahead
of Your One-Minute Manager*

Rae André, Ph.D.
Peter D. Ward, J.D.

HOUGHTON MIFFLIN COMPANY BOSTON

Library of Congress Cataloging in Publication Data

André, Rae.
The 59-second employee.

1. Personnel management.   2. Communication in
management.   3. Organizational behavior.   I. Ward,
Peter D.   II. Title.   III. Title: Fifty-nine-second
employee.
HF5549.A8527   1984   650.1′3′0207   83-18609
ISBN 0-395-35630-X

Contents

To Our Fellow Employees ... 7

In the Land of the One-Minute Manager 13

In the Real World ... 15

The One-Minute Employee? 24

When Efficient Is Inefficient 30

How to Avoid the One-Minute Reprimand 37

How to Take Advantage of the One-Minute
  Praising 48

Manage Your Manager for Fun and Profit 54

Manage Your Company for Security and
  Satisfaction 64

Manage Yourself for Respect and Growth 76

Six Pressure Points and What to Do About Them 80

The 59-Second Game Plan 88

A Message from Our Product 99

A Message to Managers 111

To Our Fellow Employees . . .

YOU ALL KNOW who we're talking about: he's the guy with the book in his briefcase and the glint in his eye. He's the One-Minute Manager, or the Theory Z Manager, or the Manager-in-Search-of-Excellence. He's the manager who's up on the latest management theory . . . and his employees are often down on him.

Why? Because a manager with a new idea is like a cook with a new recipe: whether we like it or not, he's going to dish it out. And, in the business world, it's the employees who have to eat it.

One-minute management is today's trendy new recipe for managing people. The ingredients are simple. You give forty hours of labor per week and in return they feed you these neat one-minute praisings. Or when you do anything wrong, any little thing at all, you get a one-minute reprimand that they deliver with true feeling while standing behind your desk with their arm around you.

Hey, whatever you're into.

The truth is that every *manager* needs managing ... for his own good and for the good of your company. To say nothing of your salary review. So we've got to get cooking. As employees, it's our duty to manage our managers.

We call this process *managing up*. And just like traditional management (managing down), it is an essential business strategy. Just as managing down has many goals, so does managing up. You can manage up to help yourself, you can manage up to help your boss, you can manage up to help your co-workers, or you can manage up to help your company. Whatever your goal, as employees your main job is to turn your managers into winners — because if they're losing more than they're winning they can't possibly help you, themselves, or anyone else.

59-second employees realize the importance of managing up. They strive to get a one-second jump on management—that crucial bit of time that allows them to do more than just swallow things whole. 59-second employees realize that they need to plan, that their own contribution to the company is important, and that management isn't always right.

We believe that being a 59-second employee is good for you. We also believe that it's good for your manager and good for your company. Managing up keeps an organization honest and in touch with what's really going on; it keeps it from getting flabby.

The 59-second employee manages up for fun and for profit—and for the good of the firm.

The Symbol of the
59-Second Employee
Is the Brick,
Because It's Solid,
Inexpensive,
and On the Square.

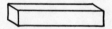

Just Like Most Employees.

In the Land of the One-Minute Manager

NOT SO LONG AGO we knew a guy who needed a job. We'll call him Dave. Dave was young, and he hadn't held too many jobs before. But he was also a skilled employee and he didn't want just any job. So Dave polished his résumé, worked his contacts, followed up on dozens of leads, and interviewed hard. After much searching, one day at an interview Dave was introduced to a one-minute manager. Dave was impressed. This manager was efficient and kind, but tough when he needed to be.

The manager liked Dave, too. He was looking for a team player. He felt that Dave would learn the lessons of one-minute management quickly and well.

Dave was sold on one-minute management. He admired a manager who had a consistent philosophy. He believed that managers should be tough, but that they should also be generous enough to give rewards when rewards were due. He thought clear and concise goal setting was essential to keep an organization pulling together. Above all, he believed that managers should be efficient. One-minute management stressed all of these ideals.

Dave had talked to several of the one-minute manager's employees and they had all agreed that one-minute management was the way to go. For him, that clinched the deal. When the one-minute manager offered Dave the job, he took it.

And so it came to pass that, using the secrets of one-minute management, Dave and his manager worked happily ever after.

For about six months.

In the Real World . . .

I T DAWNED on Dave that he had developed some serious problems with one-minute management. But he couldn't understand his feelings. He had bought into the philosophy of one-minute management 100 percent. It had made sense to him at the time. He had been eager to make it work. He had tried hard. He had been sincere. What had gone wrong?

Dave thought back over the six months, a training period during which he had spent several weeks in each of the major departments of his division. He had reported to several different managers. All except one had been one-minute managers.

Early on in the rotation, he had reported to Mr. Ketchum. Ketchum was an intelligent man, experienced and efficient, and he had recently learned to use one-minute management. "Dave," he had said to him one day, "I want to tell you what a good job you've done on the Filbert project."

Dave could see that a one-minute praising was about to be delivered.

The one-minute praising is the first secret of one-minute management. The one-minute manager strives to be on the spot when his employees are doing something right. He is always on the lookout for that moment of success, especially when he's got a new person on board. Sooner or later, the employee will do something right and the one-minute manager will make his move: He delivers the one-minute praising. The employee hears a description of what he has just done, why the manager is glowing with warm feelings about it, and how the company will prosper from the employee's actions.

Then the manager pauses. This moment of silence allows the employee to bask in the approbation he has just received. At the end of the pause, the manager urges the employee to continue the good behavior so that more good feelings can come his way. Finally, the manager touches the employee. He may pat him or her on the shoulder. He may even go so far as to shake hands. And with this gesture, the one-minute praising ends.

Being well versed in one-minute management, Dave knew the ritual of a one-minute praising. Still, even though he knew what to expect, Dave was anxious about his own first one-minute praising. How would he feel? How should he act?

Just as Mr. Ketchum was about to speak, Dave interrupted nervously, "Oh, that's not really necessary, Mr. Ketchum. I'm really only doing my—"

"Nonsense! It most certainly is necessary." And he went on for not quite sixty seconds. "There now."

When he paused, Dave said, "Why, thank you, Mr. Ketchum. It's so very kind of you to say so."

"Not at all, Dave, you deserve it. Or rather, your behavior deserves it. Or rather . . . well, you know what I mean." And he touched him lightly on the shoulder and walked off, looking perplexed, as he sometimes did.

Thinking back on it, Dave confessed to mixed feelings: "I felt, well, O.K. about it. But not great. Not super-motivated. More than a little embarrassed, actually. Mr. Ketchum followed the rules, all right. Hey, they say they've tried this out on pigeons and rats and little kids and it worked on them. Maybe there's something wrong with me."

Later that week Dave screwed up on the Phelps account. He knew exactly what he'd done wrong. He knew how to fix it next time. He also knew that Mr. Ketchum had heard about it, so when he received the phone call arranging an immediate meeting, he wasn't surprised. The cardinal principle of the one-minute reprimand is that the employee should get it right away.

The one-minute reprimand is the second secret practiced by the one-minute manager. Sooner or later, every employee is going to screw up, and the one-minute manager is on the spot when the screw-up occurs. He then delivers a precise explanation of how you have screwed up and how he as your manager feels about it. His response may be anger or disappointment or something negative, but whatever it is, he tells it like it is. Then he pauses to let you experience his feeling. Finally he gives you the touch. This lets you know that in spite of the anger, the disappointment, and the difference in your status, the manager is really on your side. He reminds you of how much he admires you, if not your behavior.

Dave knew that the one-minute manager has a reputation for "being on top of things."

"Dave, you've screwed up on the Phelps account," Mr. Ketchum began. "That's really quite unacceptable, you know. And I'm mad as hell. And disappointed in you. Don't let me catch you doing it again; we expect so much more." He paused, then walked behind the desk and stretched out his hand to Dave.

"But I still respect you as a person," he added.

"Well, ah, thank you for the feedback, Mr. Ketchum," Dave stammered.

"Not at all, Dave. You deserve it. Or rather, your behavior deserves it. Or rather... " He looked confused again.

"Yes, well, thanks again, really, Mr. Ketchum. By the way, I know what caused the problem."

"Good, Dave, glad to hear it. Nice talking to you." And before Dave could respond, Mr. Ketchum turned and walked out of the office.

"Nice talking to you," Dave mumbled.

One-minute goal setting is the third secret of one-minute management. One-minute managers pride themselves on efficiency in working with people. When they want to know their employees' goals, they ask them to write the goals down, using one piece of paper for each goal. One-minute managers have to be able to read each page in one minute or less or the process is not efficient. Also, one-minute managers believe that only about 20 percent of employees' goals are really important. So they only let employees write down about a half a dozen of all their goals. "Being a manager is not as tough as people would have you believe," one-minute managers say, "and managing people doesn't take as long as you think."

A few weeks later, Dave was rotated into a department run by Ms. Dunham, a Very Positive Person. Dunham caught Dave doing stuff right all the time. She smiled at him in the hall, invited him to lunch. Dunham even sat down in Dave's office with him and talked about Dave's goals. Dave noticed that Dunham often touched him on the shoulder when they were in a group conversation, and that she introduced him around in glowing terms. Dave loved working for Dunham, who dished up more than her share of one-minute praisings but rarely dished out one-minute reprimands.

Dave had worked hard to inform Ms. Dunham about his goals. He had spent one day just figuring out what all his goals were, and then another few days condensing all of these into a few pages. Ms. Dunham had encouraged him to include long-term career goals, as well as short-term job goals.

Then one day the letter arrived. It seemed that one

of Dave's clients had written to Ms. Dunham's boss complaining bitterly about Dave's work. Dave went straight to Dunham with his explanation, which was that there must have been a misunderstanding. Dunham, moreover, understood perfectly, and even complimented Dave on how well he had handled the complaint. Dave's fears were calmed, and following Dunham's advice, he let it drop without further action. Dunham had said, "Look, let's just forget it," and Dave had agreed.

Months went by before Dave found out the truth: he had been set up by Dunham. As Dave later figured it, Dunham had been threatened by him and his wonderful, ambitious goals. Knowing Dave's goals intimately, Dunham also knew exactly how best to thwart them, and did: now everyone in the office knew about the complaint, Dave learned, and Dunham had done nothing to stop their impression that the complaint was fully justified. Dave had been one-minute managed right into an ambush.

In his final rotation, Dave had worked for Mr. Hart, who was simply ... different. Dave didn't know exactly how to describe him. Hart was an old-timer; one-minute management seemed to have passed him by. Hart must not have been very efficient, Dave thought, because his door was always open. He spent a lot of time listening to Dave. Often he just nodded as Dave talked, and sometimes he would give an opinion. He never gave one-minute praisings or one-minute reprimands. If you did a good job, Hart might just smile when he heard about it, or if you did something really special, he might invite you in for coffee and a chat. "He doesn't have much clout around here. Still, I find it useful to try my ideas on him," Dave mused.

One day he did something wrong. Hart just ignored it. Another time Dave made an error, and when Hart heard about it, he asked him why it had turned out so badly. Together they had figured out a way to avoid the problem in the future. But Hart never got really angry. Thinking back on it, Dave realized that he had found Hart's smile very satisfying, that he had been really pleased to be invited in for coffee. He had really liked working for Hart.

Dave blushed as he thought about his earlier enthusiasm for one-minute management. That stint in Hart's department had convinced him, finally, that one-minute management wasn't for him. After all, it didn't account for Hart's management style. It didn't explain his own positive reaction to that style. One-minute management looked good on paper, but in practice, it was just too simple.

And yet here he was, employed in a company run mostly by quick-fix managers, involved in a system that almost everyone praised except himself. Dave wanted to survive in his job, but he wanted to like it too.

He was determined to do something . . . but what?

The One-Minute Employee?

THE FIRST idea that Dave had was to use the theory that he had so recently internalized. "I'll conform to the system," he decided. "Only I'll use the system on them. I'll become a one-minute employee."

For instance, he could try a one-minute praising. Well, he had tried that once, he remembered, and his boss had told him to "Cut the crap—I know when I'm being one-minute praised. Why don't you just tell me what you want?" And they had both laughed because the boss had called it exactly right, and even though Dave had honestly felt that his boss deserved the compliment, he also knew that he had wanted to accomplish something with that compliment. Dave had gone away feeling an emotion somewhere between embarrassment and frustration. No, one-minute praisings wouldn't work. One-Minute managers were highly suspicious of praise from employees.

Then Dave thought about a one-minute reprimand. Not for long though. He could just see himself telling the old one-minute manager exactly what he had done wrong and how he, peon Dave, felt about it, then pausing to let it sink in and going around to the other side of his desk and putting his hand on his manager's shoulder. Dave could just see himself telling his manager how he, Dave, really valued the manager personally, if not his behavior.

Right.

Well, then what about one-minute goal setting? I could ask my manager to write his one-minute goals for me. Then we could compare notes, Dave reasoned. But he suspected it wouldn't work. "Writing goals is your job," the manager would say. "You've been around here long enough to know that. But I do value your efforts, so keep up the good work." No, his manager had made it clear that he was not going to write the goals himself: that was inefficient. "Also safe," Dave thought.

Dave made up his mind. "If I'm going to be happy here I'm just going to have to try something different. I'm going to have to improve on the goal setting, take advantage of the praisings, and avoid the reprimands. I'm going to have to be one step ahead of these guys. If I can't join them at their game of behavior modification, I'll try to beat them."

And thus was born ...

———

The 59-Second Employee

The 59-second employee
strives to stay
one <u>significant</u> second
ahead of the
one-minute manager.

The 59-second employee
uses his extra time to
plan his strategy.

The 59-second employee
learns to manage *up.*

———

The One-Minute Manager's Philosophy Is:

———

Looks aren't everything.
Hidden inside every employee
is a person who can make it.

———

The 59-Second Employee's Philosophy Is:

———

Looks aren't everything.
Hidden inside every manager
is a person who can break it.

———

When Efficient Is Inefficient

D AVE WASN'T quite sure what being a 59-second employee was all about, but he was determined to figure it out. After his six-month training rotation, he settled down into his permanent job with his very own one-minute manager. We'll call his manager Mr. OMM.

One day Mr. OMM called Dave in for a goal-setting session. Goal setting, he reminded Dave, makes clear what your responsibilities are and what you're accountable for.

"Now this is what I want you to accomplish," OMM said, and he talked for several minutes about his goals for Dave. "Of course, according to the principles of one-minute management, the standards must be clear; they are as follows . . ."

As he talked, Dave was busy calculating. "Hmm. He's talked for about twenty minutes so far, and I guess he's talking at the rate of eighty words per minute, so that's about sixteen hundred words so far. At two hundred words per goal that should be about eight goals we should have covered by now."

Suddenly Mr. OMM stopped. "And that's about it," he said.

Dave quickly totaled it up in his head. Eight goals, sixteen hundred words. Two hundred words per goal. Wow, it certainly felt efficient. And according to the principles of one-minute management, he only had to write up six! That was easy! But he did have some questions.

Though Mr. OMM had mentioned eight goals for him, Dave had at least a dozen additional goals for himself. That made twenty. Dave was anxious about how to accomplish many of these goals — in fact he was unsure about more than half of them. And he was unsure of which were most important — his or Mr. OMM's.

He felt he knew his job better than OMM did, but how would his boss react if he left some of the boss's goals out? How was he, Dave, going to feel if he didn't get some of his goals clarified — and later was evaluated on these? And how about some of his more complicated tasks? For one thing, he knew he couldn't possibly summarize his goals and evaluation criteria for work on the new computer system in even three hundred words per goal.

"Ah, I need some clarification on a few points, Mr. OMM," he ventured.

"Certainly, my boy, go right ahead."

Dave explained his first dilemma, that goal Q represented a very complicated task. "I don't see how I can do it justice in one page, sir."

"Look, Dave, I don't want you to think I'm inflexible. I can see you're uncomfortable about it. So take, let's say, a page and a half if you like. Put in some of your own ideas. If I take two minutes to read it instead of one, so what, right? I'm a fast reader. You know my most fulfilling moments are spent working with my staff. Any other problem?"

"Well, yes, actually. I really think I have a lot of important goals. I'm sure there are more than six and —"

OMM interrupted. He sounded firm. "Let me see what you've written, according to the rules, Dave. Then we'll talk about it." He stood up, smiled, and touched Dave on the shoulder.

Dave smiled back, but when he left Mr. OMM's office his face fell. "Efficient is inefficient when it's insufficient," he thought angrily. When he got back to his desk Dave took out a notepad and wrote at the top in big black letters:

FRUSTRATIONS UNDER ONE-MINUTE GOAL SETTING

Idea 1. Under one-minute goal setting you can spend more time worrying about choosing goals and picking exactly the right words than you would if you simply wrote everything out in full.

Idea 2. The world is too complicated for a one-minute fix.

Idea 3. My job is too complicated for a one-minute fix.

And then he wrote out and underlined:

I'M MAD AS HELL AT ONE-MINUTE GOAL SETTING AND

I'M NOT GOING TO TAKE IT FOR ONE MORE SECOND!!

"Well, that feels better," he said to himself. "Now what the heck am I going to do about it?" He ripped off the first sheet, and at the top of a new page he wrote:

CREDO OF THE 59-SECOND GOAL SETTER

Dave thought a minute, then wrote rapidly:

Set your own goals first.

Then listen to your boss's goals.

Write up the six easiest goals — six that your boss will go along with.

Work on these six goals up front — and your own goals out back.

Keep trying to get your boss to really listen to you.

Dave put down his pen and thought about what he had written. Sad but real, he thought. If OMM's going to put efficiency above communication and numbers above needs, I'm just going to have to protect myself. Maybe Hart would like to listen to what I think needs to be done around here . . . I think I'll invite him to lunch.

The One-Minute Manager Says:

———

In no time at all
I get impressive results
from my people.

———

The 59-Second Employee Adds:

————

. . . As long as
your people say "squeak"
and eat cheese.

————

How to Avoid the
One-Minute Reprimand

A SHORT TIME after he had decided to become a 59-second employee, Dave was on the receiving end of a one-minute reprimand from Mr. OMM. Dave had never felt good about one-minute reprimands. "But then I'm not supposed to feel good," he reasoned. "I'm supposed to feel bad and to change my behavior accordingly."

During the reprimand, Dave managed to stay outwardly calm. But inwardly he was seething. Later, sitting in his office talking to himself he said, "Hey, you know what? I've always tried my best. And when I get punished for my mistakes, sometimes I just don't feel like trying so hard anymore. Now how useful is that to the company? Or to me?" He fantasized his revenge.

He would love to give OMM a one-minute reprimand about one-minute reprimands! He imagined how the dialogue would go:

"Mr. OMM," he would say, looking him cooly in the eye, "you know I've always told you that I want to let you know how you're doing and in no uncertain terms. Following, of course, the inviolate principles of one-minute management."

"Yes, Dave, you have." Mr. OMM would sit up straight in his chair. His eyes would widen ever so slightly.

"Well, sir, just a few minutes ago you gave me a one-minute reprimand. I am extremely angry at you for doing that, and I'm hurt. It was unnecessary and unkind. Frankly, I don't enjoy being on the receiving end of that kind of behavior. It's not what I expect from my boss, someone I'm supposed to look up to. How useful is it to punish people for trying hard? How useful is it to punish people when nobody's perfect? How useful is it —" Dave caught himself . . . he was close to sixty seconds already.

Mr. OMM would no doubt get pink in the face as Dave paused for the required few seconds of uncomfortable silence in which Mr. OMM would experience Dave's anger. Then Dave would walk up and put his hand out to OMM. OMM, red around the eyeballs, would take it mechanically. He wouldn't be able to speak.

"I really value you a lot, Mr. OMM," Dave would say. "I didn't like your behavior just now, but I do respect you as a person. O.K.? Now let's just forget it." And with that, Dave would turn, pleased with his efficient reprimand, and start to leave. As he closed the heavy wooden door behind him, he would just barely hear his boss's stuttered "You're fired!"

"Hmph. No happy ending to that fairy tale," Dave said to himself and grimaced. "One-minute reprimands are certainly not a two-way street! At least not around here!

"In reality, Mr. OMM doesn't like to be reprimanded any more than I do, and not just because I'm threatening his bossly authority. I don't think any human being likes to be yelled at. I've never known one. Maybe there's a way to avoid reprimands."

Dave first thought of trying really hard to be a perfect employee. He'd never make a mistake. He'd work extra hard. He'd ... But no. Dave knew that he was too human for that. Besides, he reasoned, business is tough today. It's going through changes all the time — changes people can't always keep up with. Overnight technology, currency and policy changes can make you look stupid and incompetent through no fault of your own. In fact, given today's pressures, human mistakes almost have to increase! "So if I can't avoid mistakes, I could always hide them. What they don't know can't hurt me."

Dave knew a lot of employees who did that. But he weighed the consequences. First of all, he had learned way back when — in business school? — that people and organizations can learn from their mistakes. And he believed that this learning was valuable, both for one's company and for oneself. And then, too, if he didn't hide his mistakes well enough, maybe he'd get a three-minute reprimand next time. (Or, like two-minute goal setting, was that against the rules?)

No, he couldn't be Mr. Perfect and he wouldn't be Mr. Sly. In the long run, neither would work for the company or for him.

Then Dave thought of Hart. Hart usually ignored mistakes or talked with him about how to avoid them next time. Hart actually seemed to put a lot of creative thinking into how to avoid giving reprimands. Oh sure, if somebody screwed up repeatedly, they were told about it — though the reprimand was gentle if they had made an honest effort to avoid their mistake. Hart put a lot of time into coaching his people, helping them learn how to avoid mistakes in the first place and how to cope with them when something did go wrong. Occasionally he had had to remove someone from a job that the person wasn't able to learn. Dave knew that people who worked for Hart respected him, and only reluctantly transferred out of his department. "And I certainly worked my butt off for him," Dave recalled with some satisfaction.

Perhaps he could tell OMM about Hart's technique of managing, but no, OMM was fully committed to one-minute management. He wasn't about to listen to a different theory just when he had trained his staff to believe in this one. "But," Dave thought, "if Hart's technique, whatever you want to call it, worked on me, maybe it will work on OMM, too."

"That's going to take some guts," Dave thought, "but it's probably worth it. Would I really want to work here if nothing changes? The answer is no. But I'm not going to ask OMM to change. I'm going to change OMM. Next time I get a one-minute reprimand, I'm simply going to ignore it."

Dave didn't get one-minute reprimands very often, but the next time he did, he carefully said nothing. When OMM, who seemed rather surprised, asked him if he had anything to say, Dave, trying his best to look pleasant but not cocky, said, "No, not really." OMM had glanced at him, ever so oddly, and then had left.

Dave was encouraged. He felt less angry than he had at other reprimands, and this in itself was an improvement. "Who needs all that high blood pressure!" he thought. He even felt like he might have influenced OMM a bit.

It was a long time until he received another reprimand. Again he listened quietly: not angry, not laughing, just not reacting. His boss seemed to have forgotten the previous reprimand, but this time he was more taken aback than before. He didn't even ask Dave whether he had anything to say, and simply ended the reprimand and left quickly.

After this, a very long time passed between reprimands. Dave knew that the next time around he would have to take the ultimate risk. It was time that OMM learn how he felt. When he received the reprimand this time, he quietly said to his boss, "I appreciate receiving your feedback on any aspect of my job, Mr. OMM, but to tell you the truth, I'm uncomfortable with one-minute reprimands. Sure I sometimes make mistakes, but I always try to do things to the best of my ability. By being angry or disappointed with me you are really punishing my sincere effort. I would be a much better worker if you would stop reprimanding me and would instead help me learn how to do things right. I'm always interested in your opinion. It's very important to me. It helps me do my job well."

Dave paused, watching OMM, who raised one eyebrow slightly.

Dave had known in advance that he would feel nervous at this point in his little speech, and he had practiced what he would say to himself as he waited for OMM's reaction. "I'm a good employee; I have established my value here. This is a small risk to take to make my job tolerable." He waited. He hoped that some of the same thoughts were going through OMM's head: "This is a good employee. He's valuable here. What the hell is he talking about?"

Outwardly, OMM responded almost as usual. "Well, don't do it again, Dave. Now let's just forget it." Yet even as his boss was delivering his habitual end-of-the-reprimand routine, Dave could see that OMM was quite puzzled, that if OMM hadn't agreed with his little speech, at least it had registered.

"We're all in this together, right, Dave?" OMM said and turned toward him.

"Yes, sir, most definitely." They shook hands and went their separate ways.

It would be misrepresenting the truth to say that Dave never received another one-minute reprimand. A management style is a management habit, and slow to change. But a couple of years later, looking back, he couldn't remember very many of them. Usually, he didn't get them at all anymore from month to month, and when he did, they were a shadow of their former selves, with less emphasis on feeling and more emphasis on problem solving. Even when he did get a particularly nasty one, one of the original variety, these days Dave took it philosophically, chalking it up to a temporary, and human, relapse in Mr. OMM's effective new management style.

About the One-Minute Reprimand,
the One-Minute Manager Says:

———

I guarantee you,
you won't forget it.

———

And the 59-Second Employee Says:

———

You bet your sweet tush
I won't.

———

If All Else Fails, the 59-Second Employee
Sends a Message:

———

Your sincere criticism is
deeply appreciated.
Screw you very much.

———

How to Take Advantage
of the One-Minute Praising

MARY ALDRICH was Mr. OMM's secretary. She got one heck of a lot of one-minute praisings! More than Dave did, more than the other secretaries did, more than anybody did. Mary always said that she and her boss had a "wonderful working relationship." Yet Dave knew from the grapevine that Mary was long overdue for a raise.

"There's a lesson in this for 59-second employees," Dave told himself. "One-minute praisings are nice, all right. And it makes sense, even to a 59-second employee, to enjoy them. However, I shouldn't let that good feeling lull me into sacrificing the critical one-second advantage! Talk, after all, is cheap. What I need to do is to translate all that good will into things that count even more — things like recognition, a more challenging job, a better office, a raise . . ."

The 59-second secret of one-minute praisings is:

DON'T SETTLE FOR THEM.
TURN THEM INTO SOMETHING CONCRETE.

Soon after he became a 59-second employee, Dave got a one-minute praising from his boss. Just as his boss was shaking his hand, Dave thanked him politely for the praise, mentioned that a seminar he wanted to attend was coming up next month, and asked him if he had made any decision on it yet.

He hadn't, but he did, and Dave was sent.

The next time Dave got a one-minute praising from someone influential outside his department, he asked her if she would put her praising into a letter to his boss. The letter arrived the following week, and went into Dave's personnel file.

The next time Dave got a one-minute praising on a project he had done, he asked, right away, whether he might present it to the next level of management.

The answer was no.

"So, you can't win them all," Dave thought. "I've got the germ of an idea here, however: two out of three is better than sitting there with a lap full of praise. The other employees are left holding a whole lot of good vibes, while the 59-second employee has a special seminar and a strong recommendation."

Dave had learned long ago how to perform. Now he was learning how to turn performance into rewards.

He was also gaining a new respect for limits. "One-minute praisings can be given to anyone," he thought, "because it is possible to give away so many. But there is only one new job opening up, and four people probably want it. There's only so much money for special projects. There's only so much opportunity for exposure elsewhere in the company. I have to decide which rewards are most important to me, and then make sure OMM, who is a manager I trust, knows what I want. And I'm also going to have to live with the idea that, because we're a true work team here, some of these rewards will have to be shared."

Dave decided not to ask for something every time he got a praising. He didn't want to punish people for giving him rewards! And he decided that sometimes it might not be a good idea to ask for the reward right after the praising. Doing that once in a while looks assertive and eager. ("And, indeed," Dave thought, "I am!") Doing it often looks pushy. It is possible to ask for too much.

Dave saw many possibilities ahead. "It's almost as

if the one-minute praising has been set up to challenge an employee's creativity and initiative in thinking up other rewards. But no, it couldn't be." He chuckled. "Only a 59-second employee would be crazy enough to think that."

Thus it was that with ingenuity, flexibility, and a basic understanding of his boss as a human being, Dave finally found his niche. And worked happily ever after.

The One-Minute Manager Says:

————

Think about your goals.
Consider how well
you do your job.
See if your abilities
match your aspirations.

————

The 59-Second Employee Says:

___

. . . Then ask for a raise.

___

(Or whatever!)

Manage Your Manager for Fun and Profit

MANAGERS HAVE all the fun, or so their management books tell them. They get to decide what's going on here, they're told. They get to make people do stuff, *their* stuff. They get to choose a management style from a whole shopping list of possibilities: a style that's more or less participative, a style that's more or less formal, a style that's more or less rewarding.

But, as Dave has shown us, 59-second employees can play the game too. They know that they can manage up because they know that they control some of the praisings and rewards that their managers want. Praisings and rewards like:

- being on time
- increasing productivity

- doing their job without much supervision
- smiling instead of grumping around
- delivering a high-quality product
- praising their manager to his or her boss
- supporting their manager with other employees
- giving their manager high scores on the annual personnel survey

And 59-second employees know they control some punishments, too:

- interrupting
- being late for meetings
- reducing output
- playing stupid, forcing the boss to do the work
- griping directly to their boss
- griping to their fellow employees
- griping to their boss's boss
- giving their boss low scores on the annual personnel survey
- starting a union drive
- talking about a union drive
- thinking about a union drive
- and you can think of dozens more

Also, just like the boss, employees can adopt a managing up style that represents their personal preference of ways to manage their managers. They can be Theory X employees — tough, gruff, and uncommunicative; or Theory Y employees — cooperative, communicative, positive. In the terms of the 59-second employee, they can choose the mix of praisings and reprimands that they will use with their bosses.

A 59-second employee knows that managing up requires, above all, subtlety. A manager has direct control over the most important rewards and punishments in an organization — the money and the promotions and the rotten assignments and the varieties of corporate exile. In contrast, the employees' control is indirect.

Also, they have to be more clever about control than managers do, because the company and many of the other employees believe that managers' control is legitimate and that employees' is not. 59-second employees' power to manage up is often viewed with suspicion. It's simply "not done," which is why you've never heard about it before. But of course it is done, all the time. For these reasons, 59-second employees know they have to be cautious, but they also know that they're not powerless.

A basic tenet of managing up is that managers are human beings too; that they set goals and react to praisings and reprimands just like lowlier creatures;

that they have the same problems at home, the same confusions about life, and before a big presentation, the same nervous stomach.

Beneath the one-minute mottos, managers are normal people, and the principles of human behavior apply to them, too. They're going to set goals for themselves and their work — though of course they feel no responsibility to communicate all of the goals to you, the employee. They're going to respond positively to praisings — though they probably got ahead partly by taking advantage of them. And, like employees, they're going to try to avoid reprimands.

As a 59-second employee your strategy is to study your manager. Where does he want to go and what does he want to accomplish? How does he like to be rewarded and what's particularly punishing for him? All of this information is straightforward enough, but gathering it is not easy. If your manager were to ask *you* about such things, you'd be likely to answer truthfully, on the theory that he can't help you if you don't say what you want. But if you ask your manager these questions, he'll be likely to avoid them.

Since you're telling the truth, why shouldn't your manager do the same? Consider this example. Let's say your manager places a priority on accomplishing

X, while he manages three employees who each work on different projects, X, Y, and Z. If he tells you all that X is his main goal, the employees working on Y and Z are likely to feel slighted. They will suspect, probably accurately, that they won't be rewarded as well as the folks on project X, and they may even neglect their own work in order to jockey for entry jobs on project X. So the manager is mum about his priorities, and rambles on vaguely about teamwork, corporate philosophy, and one big happy family. Sound familiar?

Of course, if managers have good reasons for secrecy, 59-second employees have even better reasons for wanting to know. And they will go to great lengths to find out as much about their manager as possible. Here strategy will take many forms. The employee can ask the manager directly, of course, and possibly get a small amount of guarded information. Better yet, the employee can spend a little less effort trying to impress the boss and a little more time watching for clues. At meetings, conferences, and performance reviews, the employee can ask the manager for his view on project Q. He can spend as much informal time with his manager as possible, hoping for helpful hints. Once on the golf course, the employee can ask the manager what his views on project Q *really* are. He can talk, talk, talk with everybody he can find who knows the boss. More to the point, he can listen, listen, listen.

Your success at managing your boss depends on the quality and currency of information that you obtain, so keep at it. Like managing down, it's a task that never goes away. But then what should you do with the information once you've got it?

First, size up your boss in terms of how he actually reacts. Maybe your boss is the type who always greases the squeaky wheel, who deals with problem employees first (probably to avoid conflict) and pays much less attention to other employees. The 59-second employee who wants to get promoted out of a department will squeak at the pitch the boss hates the most.

Most bosses, like most of us, will be less obvious and will react to a mixture of rewards and punishments. The 59-second employee's job is to figure out what mixture works. For example, take positive feedback. Sure it's a good idea. But there are limits. When does the boss start to feel that your positive feedback is turning into brown-nosing? Can he stand positive feedback daily? Weekly? Every time you see him?

Every third time? Eighth time? Will he respond only if you praise him in front of peers? Or only if you're alone with him? Perhaps he won't respond to positive feedback much at all, and will respond only to other rewards that you can provide, such as high output or being on time. (This is, however, unlikely.)

Can your boss take criticism from you, an employee? How often, in what way, on what subjects, would he be willing to take criticism without feeling that you've overstepped your bounds? Some managers react badly to any criticism whatsoever ... on the other hand, some react badly only when they don't get the kind of negative feedback that they consider critical to their own improvement and to their company's success.

Consider all of these alternatives. Test them, if at all possible, by taking small steps at first. Start by giving mild negative feedback and watching your manager's reactions carefully. Try different mixes, over time, until you find the blend that allows you to manage up most efficiently with this particular manager. If you change managers, you have to start the learning process again.

In all of this, your style of managing up is important. If you're a Theory X employee, having learned that you've got to be tough with management or they'll be tough with you, you may not be able to adjust to a positive manager. Or maybe you're a Theory Y employee, one who has learned that a participative, cooperative style usually gets results. If so, you'll be miserable in a Theory X setting. You should either change your style to match your manager's or move on.

Just as management has to make decisions on whether satisfaction leads to productivity and whether satisfaction is therefore worthy of investment, so the employee has to decide whether a managing up style is going to lead to better pay, a more challenging job, or whatever it is that he wants most. Just as a sound business judges prospective employees, so the employee will get the information he needs to judge his manager.

As anyone who has studied managing down knows, these choices are never easy. Human systems are so complicated that the data are seldom indisputable. Employees have even less data on their managers than their managers have on them. And every new manager represents a new experiment.

59-second employees know managing up is seldom easy. But they believe that it is almost always useful.

The One-Minute Manager Says:

———

Employees are
more than what they do.
They are the people
behind what they do.

———

The 59-Second Employee Knows:

———

Employees are
more than what they do.
Employees are
their managers' perceptions
of what they do.

———

Manage Your Company for Security and Satisfaction

ONCE YOU DECIDE to manage up, you've got a fundamental choice to make. You can decide to manage your company and protect your future, or you can decide to ignore your company now and risk losing your job, your financial support, and your sanity later. It's as simple and as complicated as that.

"What, me manage the company? I'm nowhere near the top," you say.

Your humility is well taken. You are an employee. In some companies you're just-an-employee. And, taken together, all of the employees of a company are still just-the-employees. Employees are rather low on the pecking order of assets, if you can think of it that way — somewhere below liquid assets and good will and somewhere above the copying machine. Maybe.

So what can managing your company possibly

mean? It means that your company is you. It's you in a very small but important way. You're only one part of the whole, but at the same time the whole is equal to the sum of its parts.

One way to manage the company from below is to realize that companies are made up of coalitions. Company goals are the goals of the strongest coalitions, or the goals achieved by compromise among coalitions. As an employee you can see yourself as a loner and only take from the company what rewards it has to give, or you can see yourself as a member of a coalition and work with that coalition to influence the future direction of the company. You can join coalitions, create coalitions, lead coalitions. A good start is the realization that there's a great deal more to organizational politics than the organizational chart would indicate.

Perhaps you're a dispensable part of your company — one person with one job that can easily be filled by somebody else. In that case, another way to improve your ability to manage up to the company level is to get yourself out of the dispensable job and into an indispensable one, so that everyone gets the idea that they'll have to continue to deal with you — permanently.

A third way to manage up, the rarist and most risky, is simply to have the courage and ability to say what you believe, and of course, enough security to face the real possibility of losing your job.

During the 1982 recession-depression we attended a conference where we listened to a large group of personnel administrators being told that a great way to cut costs is to fire a lot of middle managers. "You'd be surprised how many of them will appreciate it in the long run," the speaker told the group. "And, of course, top management would appreciate it on the bottom line right now." The personnel managers, to a man and woman, embraced this idea without question. We were struck by the fact that not one of them mentioned that perhaps these middle managers would like to have a voice in the matter. Yet we're sure that many of the personnel administrators are truly humane individuals, at least part time.

Certainly, managing the company from below is harder than managing your manager from below. You have even less information, and less access to rewards and punishments. Furthermore, as the example just given makes clear, values are set at the top of an organization. Morality moves down the corporate ladder but seldom up. The group of personnel administrators accepted the profit motive as the dominant, even the sole, motive of their respective companies. They ignored the company's responsibility to its employees and to the greater community. They've obviously decided that to do otherwise is too risky.

So as a 59-second employee, you really have your job cut out for you.

Why should you bother to manage up to influence your company?

For starters, you need to know where the company is going so that you can adjust your own educational and job goals to match. You also want to influence the company's direction so it continues to include you as a valued member. Finally, you're doing the company a service by giving it the opportunity to take full advantage of your talents and ability to grow.

Managing up can help you, the 59-second employee, to establish whether top management is on the level when they say that employees are important to the company. Being informed will allow you to judge *how* important. Important until the next recession hits? Important until the president wants to move the corporate offices to Tampa? Or important enough to make the company establish, for instance, a true no-layoff policy? Being a conscious coalition member will help you contribute to the meaningful resolution of such questions.

In the best of companies the expressed policy is "we are all in this together." Yet, the prevailing attitude among many employees about their company today (to borrow an expression from the sixties) is "Love it or leave it." The 59-second employee takes still a different attitude toward the company: "Change it or lose it."

The One-Minute Manager Says:

————

Employees who are
bullish about themselves
are bullish about
their company.

————

The 59-Second Employee Says:

—

Employees who are
bullish about their company
are bullish about
themselves.

—

The One-Minute Manager Says:

———

Employees who
see themselves as first-rate
produce work
that's first-rate.

———

The 59-Second Employee Says:

——

Employees who
think that their <u>company</u>
is first-rate
produce work
that's first-rate.

——

The One-Minute Manager Says:

———

Get bullish
about your employees.
Catch them
doing something right.

———

The 59-Second Employee Says:

———

Get bullish
about your company.
Catch it doing something
for the community.

———

———

We are more than
our behavior.
We are our
company's behavior.

———

Manage Yourself for Respect and Growth

Y OU JUST spent two months with your company's external auditors . . . or two days doing the quarterly inventory. But when was the last time you took two hours to do a personal audit? Not the dollars and cents kind of audit, not your bookkeeping and your finances and your checkbook balancing, but an audit of your goals and your values and your personal achievements — the debits and credits of the real business of life?

A good manager takes the task of people management seriously, and devotes a significant proportion of work time to it. A 59-second employee will too. But do you do the same thing for yourself? Have you taken the time you need to manage yourself well? Or have you gotten so tied up with daily tasks that you've "temporarily" put aside your personal planning?

As a 59-second employee, use some of your time to manage yourself. Keep a set of personal books — anything from an extensive diary about who you are and where you're going to a doodle-book with a few notes jotted down. See where you're in the red or the black, and figure out how to do better next quarter, and next year.

Do a periodic personal audit. Ask other people for feedback. Are you still moving in the direction in which you want to move? Do you seem happy to them? Do they think that the goals you've set are still right for you?

And make time for personal development — time to learn more about your own potential, time to plan for personal long-range changes.

Keep an eye on the bottom line, but not so diligently that you fail to enjoy yourself along the way. In short, manage yourself, for increased self-respect and growth.

The One-Minute Manager
Is
"Quite a Guy."

The 59-Second Employee
Is
Too.

Six Pressure Points
and What to Do About Them

Managing up is naturally going to be easier when things are going smoothly — when your manager handles mostly routine matters in routine ways, when conflict is at a minimum. But things don't always move along on an even keel — and when conflict rocks the boat, the 59-second employee wants to have a best guess about which way to lean.

In managing up, you will face many conflict situations, situations in which you and your manager, or you and somebody up there, are at odds. We're going to point out six of the most likely pressure points here. Recognizing them is the first step toward coping.

1. The No-Win Request
Routine is when your boss asks you to do something, and you do it. Pressure is when your boss asks

you to do something, somebody else up there asks you to do something totally different, and you stew in it. When contradictory requests are made of you, you're caught: you simply can't please both sides.

As victim of the no-win request, you have to first figure out the problem. Is it that the formal chain of command has never been clarified? Is it that the formal chain of command has simply been ignored? Or has the formal chain of command been deliberately subverted? Just possibly, you're so talented that everybody up there wants you and is willing to go beyond formality to get you.

Another possibility, of course, is that somebody up there hates you and is willing to go beyond formality to get *at* you ...

Whatever the scenario, you've got your standard responses to choose from: like your animal ancestors, you can choose to fight or you can choose to flee. As a 59-second employee, of course, you can also choose to ignore. Every situation is different, so we're reluctant to give wholesale advice. But it does make common sense that if this problem comes up once, it may perhaps be safely ignored ... More than once and you should probably take steps to deal with it.

2. *Your Goals Versus Their Goals*

An organization is made up of a group of people who have some goals in common and some goals not in common. Having some goals that are different from your organization's goals is therefore normal.

A 59-second employee will, first of all, be very clear about his or her personal goals. Joining an organization means compromising some of these, but maximizing others. The pressure comes when goals that you want to maximize turn out to be minimized by your boss or your organization.

Many engineers, for example, want maximum challenge from their jobs. They want innovative, complex problems to work on. When they're assigned to work on projects that they think are unnecessary, they resent them. And, as the high turnover rates for technical employees may indicate, they often do something about this pressure. Sometimes, an employee can happily alter his goals to meet those of the organization; sometimes he can manage up to adjust those goals to more closely match his own; sometimes he has to move on. Naturally, the 59-second employee will assess the options.

3. *Your Values Versus Their Values*

In a classic study, researchers looked at the attitudes of union workers who were promoted into management. Sure enough, after their promotions, the former workers became much less pro-union. But that wasn't the end of it: as it turned out, a financial setback in the company forced many of these supervisors back into the ranks of workers, and over time, their attitudes once again became pro-union. The moral is that people will tend to adopt the values of the role in which they find themselves. The question is: how much do we really want to change? People whose values differ from the values of others in the same role are under pressure: the pro-union manager, for instance, or, not to be neglected, the employee who sticks up for management. Because of the pressure, psychologists tell us, their beliefs are likely to become more like the beliefs they see around them.

How much do we want to be influenced by outside beliefs? Each person has to decide. At the very least, the 59-second employee is extremely sensitive to values in the workplace; he knows that if you can't lick 'em, you'll probably join them.

4. Your Manager's Manager, and Others Like Him
Receiving conflicting messages from higher-ups is bad enough. Messages from your boss's boss, especially when designed to get around your boss, are sure to be no-win requests. The pressure is made worse if the messages come from especially prestigious, authoritative folks — a vice president or a plant manager or the CEO. The axiom is that the more prestigious and authoritative the message-sender, the higher the blood pressure of the employee.

We're not sure that knowing this will help, but we're sure that not knowing it will hurt: a 59-second employee will remember that the bigger they are, the harder you fall.

5. Where Confusion Reigns
Organization. The word itself means clarity and systems and order. The reality ... well, the reality of an organization may be a little different. Are your job duties unclear? Do you fail to understand fully what's expected of you? Do you lack clear authority to carry out your job responsibilities? Do you feel that you can't relate your job goals to the overall goals of the organization? Welcome to the reality of organizations, where no system is perfect and some systems are less

perfect than others. Some confusion is to be expected. The 59-second employee knows that all confusion leads to pressure. Your manager's job is to clarify; yours is to help him to clarify.

6. Work Overload

There are at least two kinds of work overload. First, there is an overload in the amount of work you have to do. Are you taking too much work home? Failing to finish what you're asked to finish, even though you're working hard? Feeling that all those meetings are taking you away from what you really need to do?

Second, there is overload in the type of work you have to do. You're overloaded if you consistently feel that unreasonable demands are being made of you, that jobs are too complex or difficult for you to do well, that you don't have enough training to do your job effectively, or that your boss expects too much from you.

That too-much-already feeling is the pressure ...

What can be done about the pressure? From management's perspective, pressure may lead to low job satisfaction, low performance, high turnover. To the employee, it may mean anything from occasional doldrums to chronic hypertension. As we have said, the first step in dealing with pressure is to recognize it. 59-second employees will not only be aware of these six common pressure points, but they will also be on the lookout for other pressure points in their jobs.

There are several options for coping with the pressure once it is recognized. You can try to control your environment or you can try to change yourself, or both. A lot has been written about stress management, mostly from the self-change point of view — deep muscle relaxation, cognitive coping, meditation, and regular exercise can all help. The 59-second employee should by all means have these basic techniques at hand.

Much less has been written about the positive effects of helping employees control their environment, though we think this may be just as important. The techniques of managing up — managing your manager, managing your company — will help because, if they're done well, they allow you to have some real control over the environment. By managing up, you can improve communications with your managers. You can encourage them to reduce confusion, or to alleviate the work overload, or to compromise on different values and goals. Using the techniques of managing up, you can influence your environment so that it really does place less stress on you.

And managing up can help in another way too. It can give employees a personal sense of mastery, control, or accomplishment. This sense of control has been used to explain, for example, why exercise reduces stress. Yes, of course, exercise may help you feel physically more relaxed, but also, meeting the challenge of exercising may be psychologically encouraging. It can give you a sense of self-esteem that in itself makes you feel less tense. For employees who may previously have felt powerless, managing up can have the same positive results. It can help you feel in control, and therefore reduce the effects of stress in your life.

The 59-Second Game Plan

GAME PLANS are made to be broken. So as a 59-second employee, keep yours simple and flexible.

Your first move is the one-second jump, the extra time that you use to anticipate and plan. You should be aware of what the psychologists call "process"; be aware that there is a pattern to the things that happen to you. The pattern is that some people tend to be more and some less supportive of you personally, that others tend to be more tolerant of your way of doing things, that still others tend to be more interested in what happens to you in the long run, and so on. Managers learn to influence this pattern for their own ends, and so does the 59-second employee. Based upon what you know about the different attitudes and abilities of the people around you, figure out how things usually get done in your organization and then develop your own strategy for getting things done for you.

Your second move should be to size up your job in terms of what's funny-enjoyable-satisfying about it and what's not-so-funny-threatening-annoying about it.

If your job is on the funny-enjoyable-satisfying side, you will enjoy it and maybe encourage more work like it. You'll tell people when you have particularly liked a project or when you've particularly enjoyed working with someone. Presumably this is why you came here to work in the first place, so you'll let people know when you're happy with your job.

But if your job is on the not-so-funny-threatening-annoying side, you should go to work on it. And in this case, your next move should be to learn about the problem. Get as much information as you can about the issue: how does it affect you, specifically? Do you contribute to the problem in some way? How does your boss see it? Who else cares about it? What has the boss done about it in the past? How does the company see it? What are the short-term and the long-term consequences to you? Your boss? The company? You get the idea...

Of course, generating the questions is easy, but

finding the answers is hard. People are suspicious of learners. "What does he want that information for?" they ask themselves. "Who does he think he is? Just because he's got an M.B.A. (read: trained to learn)! He must be ambitious; watch out!" Some companies even go so far as to discourage learning, developing "need to know" policies that restrict information access unless an employee demonstrates a need to know. And though these policies are designed, quite reasonably, to protect trade and company secrets, they can spill over into the daily business of the employees, where they establish inhibiting norms of secrecy.

The 59-second employee has to learn how to learn. Subtlety is your specialty. Learn to lead discussions rather than to ask questions. Learn who knows what, and where and when they like to talk about it. Learn to observe rather than to chatter. And even if there's nothing special going on, keep on learning, just in case.

Finally, information in hand, the 59-second employee makes a decision on what to do. You understand your position in the organization. You have mastered the different ways of managing up. And the choice is yours. Of course in making the choice, you would be wise to consider an important new discovery made by a long-lost tribe of idealistic aboriginals, and recently revealed by organizational researchers from a major university. The evidence shows that this tribe spent several centuries refining its organization. It worked on structure and strategy, selection and training, markets and operations. In the fourth century of experimentation the tribe finally decided it had found the ultimate secret of organization. In celebration, it inducted all of its members under a new name: henceforth they were to be known as the Tanobway tribe.

The tribal secret of the Tanobway? It is the ironclad law that "There Ain't No One Best Way."

Or, as our philosophical 59-second employee is likely to say, "I'll make my own best guess, and then see how it goes."

The 59-Second Game Plan

FIGURE OUT WHAT'S FUNNY AND
WHAT'S NOT-SO-FUNNY ABOUT YOUR JOB.

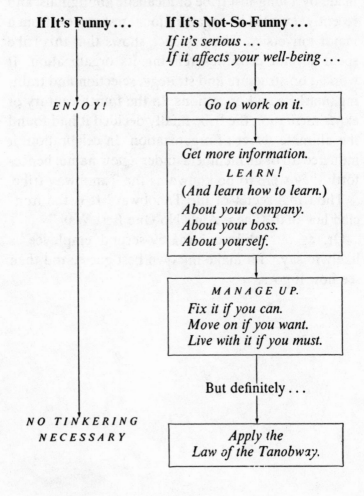

If It's Funny ...   **If It's Not-So-Funny ...**

If it's serious ...
If it affects your well-being ...

ENJOY!

> Go to work on it.

> *Get more information.*
> *LEARN!*
> *(And learn how to learn.)*
> *About your company.*
> *About your boss.*
> *About yourself.*

> *MANAGE UP.*
> *Fix it if you can.*
> *Move on if you want.*
> *Live with it if you must.*

But definitely ...

NO TINKERING
NECESSARY

> *Apply the*
> *Law of the Tanobway.*

The One-Minute Manager Says:

———

My most fulfulling moment
is the one I share
with my employees.

———

The 59-Second Employee Says:

_____

My most fulfilling moment
is the one I spend
psyching out my boss.

_____

Or . . .

———

**Getting the company
to see beyond
the quarterly report.**

———

Or . . .

___

Covering my ass.

___

Or if all else fails . . .

Translating my résumé
into Japanese.

The 59-Second Employee Always Remembers:

———

The Law of the Tanobway*

———

* "There ain't no one best way." (Only people who wish
there were — and don't we all!)

A Message from Our Product

O NCE UPON a time there was a widget. A weird widget. The widget was weird because, unlike most widgets, he was all alone. He yearned to be manufactured by the hundreds and thousands so that he would never be alone again.

One day the widget had an extraordinarily widgety idea: he would find a manufacturer to reproduce him. So he got in his car and drove to the nearest industrial park. The widget inspected the many modern buildings. Some looked efficient, some looked busy, some looked both efficient and busy. How would he choose the right company? he wondered.

"I know," he decided, "I will talk to the managers. And I will find the very best manager, the one who will make the best and the most widgets."

So the widget made appointments to meet the main

manager in each of the three tidiest and busiest companies.

The next day Widget arrived at the office of the first manager, a bright young man with an M.B.A. and a lot of enthusiasm.

"Hi there," said the widget.

"Hi there, yourself," said the Enthusiastic Manager, looking up from his CRT. "How are you today? Ah, I can see for myself that you are 40 by 44 centimeters, with a random access memory, a per unit cost of $97.50 and a profit margin of 24 percent. How's that!"

"I'm horribly impressed by the specifications," said the widget. "Now tell me what you know about quantity."

"Oh, that's easy," said the manager. "We put out an average of 7 widgets per minute, 420 per hour, 3150 per working day. Allowing for an average of 1.3 work stoppages and 9 holidays per year, we project a total profit margin of 34 percent, an increment of 9 percent over last year and 14 percent over the year before that."

"Ahem." The widget cleared his tubes. "I see. Most interesting. And what do you know about quality?"

"I'm pleased to be able to answer your questions

with the latest figures, Mr. W. Our quality rating year to date has been 9.4 of 10. Last year it was 9.5 and the decade average is 9.47."

"You seem to be very interested in numbers."

"Got to have the facts, yes sir! Business today runs on information, Mr. W.!"

"Yes, I can certainly see that. Thank you so much for the information."

That afternoon the widget waddled into the oldest of the three plants he had chosen, and met with a man who turned out to be the oldest of the three managers he was to meet. He was a Crusty Old Manager, and his face and his leather chair were dusty and creased.

The C.O.M. greeted Widget with a firm handshake. "What's a nice widget like you doing in a place like this?" The widget blushed and got right to the point. "I'm looking for a manager who will make some widgets: the best and the most that it's possible to make. Can you do anything for me?"

"Why we've been making things like you since before you were born. We're the most experienced in the business. We've been doing the same kind of work since before the war. Of course we can help you out."

"What can you tell me about your production capacity?"

"Production capacity? Well, we always meet our customers' needs, Widget. I ride my people if I have to to get the product out, but that's not needed very often — I'm known as tough but fair. We know by experience just how much we can produce, and we've never let a man down yet."

"And how about quality?"

"Widget, I'll give it to you straight. I'm a particular guy, and I use our products myself. I hope that recommendation is good enough for you, because it's the best I've got. We've been making widgets, and selling them too, for a long time. Trust me."

The widget stood up and shook the man's hand. "Thank you so much for your frankness," he said politely, and left for his third appointment.

"Mr. P. is out on the floor," the receptionist told him at the third plant. "He'll be over in the finishing section."

"Then we're not to meet in his office?"

"Oh no, Mr. P. almost never meets in his office. You see, he believes in the theory of management by walking around, and he's almost always out on the floor."

"Well, that's interesting," the widget thought.

"That seems to be, somehow, closer to what I want
..."

"Hello there! You must be Widget!" P. was having
a cup of coffee with one of his supervisors. He excused
himself and proceeded to walk around with Widget.
"Yes, I am. I've come to ask you a few questions
about producing widgets like me. Do you have a minute?"

"Sure, be glad to. How do you like our operation?"

"Well, I haven't seen much of it — but the people
seem pretty happy."

"Hey, glad you noticed! You see, I believe in managing by walking around. Some folks have even nick-
named me Mr. People."

Widget laughed appreciatively. "What do you do
while you're walking around?"

"Well, I get to know my people and they get to
know me. We're a pretty good group, if I do say so
myself. Take Edwards there."

Widget noted an operator, sitting in front of a lathe
and smoking a cigarette.

"We have coffee together every afternoon. Shoot
the breeze. I believe in spending time with every one
of my employees every week."

"That's nice. What can you tell me about your quantity?"

"Well, my people tell me they're on schedule, and I haven't heard anything to the contrary from upstairs. We're doing just fine."

"And how's your quality?"

"We always meet the specs. And nobody's told me we need to work on it. I'd say we're doing just fine. Oh, here's Joe — great guy, always good for a few laughs. Joe! Meet Widget!"

"Howdyado. Hey, didya hear the score of the game, Mr. P.?"

"Hah, Joe, I told you so, didn't I!"

"Yes sir, you sure did. What about that double play in the fourth inning, huh?"

"That was a great one all right."

The widget was not into baseball, and since he had learned all he could from Mr. P., he soon decided to leave.

Outside, he waddled up to a small park at the end of the street and perched on the only bench. "A seriously unproductive day," he thought. And he mechanically reviewed the conversations he had had. Each manager had had a unique approach — information, experience, or people. Each had seemed reasonably knowledgeable, in his own way. But ... there was something missing. The widget sighed.

Pretty soon a woman came along, sat on the other end of the bench, and began eating a sandwich. She said, "Hello!"

"Hello," responded Widget absent-mindedly. Not one of the managers suited him, he calculated furiously. None had convinced him that he knew what he was doing. How should he choose? The woman coughed politely.

"Oh, pardon me," he continued. "I don't mean to be rude but I've just been doing some thinking. Do you work around here?"

"Yes, I do. I'm an employee of the W company. We make wudgets." She pointed toward one of the older buildings in the park, one that Widget had ignored before.

"That's interesting ..." It wasn't really. Widget was tired and frustrated, and only wanted to be polite.

"Very interesting. I love my work. You know, wudgets are a lot like widgets. Begging your pardon, a wudget has a certain feel to it. When I put a part into a half-finished wudget, I know from years of doing it whether it's a good part or a bad part and whether the wudget is sized to accept it properly. I have little ways of testing it — finding a smooth place here, making a calibration there — to see whether it meets my standards. I really know a lot about it. And I make a great wudget. I'm sorry I'm running on so. I get enthused about my work sometimes."

Something in her words made Widget pay attention.

"Actually work with wudgets, eh?" he asked her.

"Oh, yes, I build wudgets from the bottom up. Just between you and me, I keep an eye out so Materials doesn't slip me any bad metal."

"Actually know what goes into them. And you put them together, too, eh?"

She nodded.

"You must know a lot about wudgets. Just how many wudgets do you make?"

"Not too many. I never let a wudget go off my table unless it's right, or unless my supervisor takes it. I almost always make the rate, but then nobody's perfect, right? I figure that if people really need wudgets, and it's my job to make them, I'll make whatever is needed. As good as I can, as fast as I can. I work overtime when I can. Wouldn't you, in this day and age? Hey, I gotta go. Sorry to bend your ear."

"On the contrary, it's been nice talking to you. You're an employee of —?"

"The W Company. Drop in and see us! I'll show you my wudgets."

"Thanks. I think I will." Well, she seems to know what she's talking about, Widget thought. She actually makes wudgets. I certainly will go visit that plant.

And the next day he did.

Soon after Widget arrived, the top management of the W Company set up interviews for him with some of the employees so he could find out what he needed to know. And they really knew their wudgets — how to make them, take them apart, fix them, and make them work. Widget found out that many of the employees had the same attitudes toward quality and quantity as the woman in the park. Between their knowledge and their attitudes, Widget was impressed by these employees. "Of course, their management is O.K., too," he added to himself. It didn't take long for Widget to decide to give the company his contract for 100,000 widgets.

Leaving the company headquarters after signing the contract, Widget mused to his lawyer, "You know,

I didn't really give those other companies a fair shake. I've learned something here: when it comes to the nuts and bolts of widgetry, it's the employees, not management, who really know what's going on. Employees are the people I should have been talking to in every single company, but in those other companies I never did interview any. I didn't figure it out, and management never suggested it. And who knows, they might have been top notch." He shrugged. "No ... I really didn't give those other guys a fair shake. But, I guess that's business."

And so it is.

The One-Minute Manager Says:

———

Help your employees to
help the company.
Catch them
doing something right.

———

The 59-Second Employee Says:

———

Help your managers to
help the company.
Catch them
doing something.

———

A Message to Managers

59-second employees
are the
smartest employees
you've got.

If you reward them,
they'll reward you.

Just remember,
you were probably
one yourself.

———

And That's It,
Fellow Employees.
We Hope You've Enjoyed
Reading Our Little Book
as Much as
We've Enjoyed Writing It.
Always Remember Our Symbol,
the Brick . . .
and Drop It on Your Friends.

———